DAUGHTER DAYS

JULIA WENDELL

UNSOLICITED
PRESS

Attention schools and businesses: for discounted copies on large
orders, please contact the publisher directly.

For information contact:
Unsolicited Press
Portland, Oregon
www.unsolicitedpress.com
orders@unsolicitedpress.com
619-354-8005

Cover Design: Kathryn Gerhardt
Editor: Kristen Marckmann
ISBN: 978-1-963115-34-5

For all of us daughters

Contents

DAUGHTER DAYS

JULIA WENDELL

Notes, 1969

You're so distant
in your bell bottom jeans and green Nehru jacket,
the one Mother buys for you on a foray at Nord's,
farmers and bankers and Amish
moving silently up and down the steep gray streets of
    Jamestown,
heads bowed and tunneling inward.
"Your grandfather drove buggies like that,"
she says blithely,
before lunch at the Towne Club—
chef salad and ice cream with pecan chocolate sauce—
and a quick stop in the ladies' room.
You will never be the same,
after discovering the dark
flower blossoming on your underwear.
You are excited to share the news,
already 14, worry turns to relief turns
to the beginning of a future
of the always encroaching.
What would I have you take back?
All the rushing, I suppose,
from one milestone to the next.
It's not like you can take another bite

of that ice cream, or whisper
in your lost mother's ear,
"I think I've started my period."

Choice

In another life
I'll spoon for you sliced peaches
from a stainless cup.
I'll plait violets
into your chestnut hair.

But in this life, the one that matters now,
I see a woman in the plate glass
ordering me to move.
Stepping into the field of vision
of the infra-red sensor,
electronic doors slide open.
I step back quickly
and they close.
A face in the clinic glass,
resembling mine, whispers—
"All you have to do is to walk through."

I turn back
toward Baltimore,
waiting for the man who left me here
(office building windows
glinting like cheap sunglasses).

So many cars,
so many partially-lived lives
pass me by.

I turn again
toward the membrane of glass.
Tadpole, unfinished thought
that went astray, you're nothing.
You're barely nothing.
They say the heart is beating now,
but it's so small I can't hear it.
You're a mistake the hollow in me made,
you're my belly swelling with doubt.

Suddenly, he's there, the pressure
of his hand at the small of my back,
my self-assured, resolute guide.
Together, we glide
through the clinic doors,
parting as if by magic,
making everything that just happened
disappear.

History

The children I have chosen not to have
float high above a stand of poplar.

It's March, and I've brought shoots of forsythia
inside, forcing them to bloom.
I tend to and admire them,
the children I chose.

From my midnight balcony—
a tiny figure teases the moonlight
at wood's edge. Darting
from tree to shadowy tree, she glances up
and smiles at me,
having once been banished from my body.

Adrift

With breath sour from sleep,
they join us in our sloop of wool and linen
that sways gently, taking on the extra cargo.
The long night breaks along the drowsy shore.

They have not yet learned
to scan the weather and hour,
to let the dog out, and so on,
caring only as they do for the lapping

of water, the rattle of frigate birds,
the sudden leap of flying fish. Slipping
under the white sail,
I take them back into the warmth
of my body.

The sun climbs up the sky, though it is not
yet shining in their sleep,
their world still cradled by kindness,
the most transient of human seas.

Tilling the Grave

A man trundles across the snow the red rototiller
purchased for work in kinder weather.
It is the only thing he knows
that can loosen the earth this time of year.

He tills and tills the way he does to plant
until the brick-hard loam begins to crumble
until he is able to stomp the shovel into it
to fashion the hole. Still, the shepherd is huge.

So, he digs some more, until his back begins to throb
until his neighbor trudges through the bare woods
to assure he has dug deep enough.

He drives off to collect her
from the vet's freezer,
then instructs his wife to keep the children inside
until he can get her just right.

He drags the stiffened animal
across the lawn on a tarp,
wipes the blood from her mouth and ass,
bends her legs so she will fit,

props up her ears, and closes her mouth
to belie the teeth bared against her end,
and a bone goes in beside her.

Then he calls them, he calls his family out.

And so we go down to the grave through the rain,
my 5-year-old son's chest heaving,
as his little sister fidgets in my arms.

My husband lowers each of his children
into the earth in turn
to touch the dog, then leans into his hoe

the way he does among the tomato vines,
before pushing clay and loam onto the matted fur.

In the Pasture of Dead Horses

Light rain, and I'm car-bound,
fiddling with my keys,
watching my helmeted children

repeat themselves on the backs of saddled ponies
circling a weather-worn ring
north of Baltimore.

So around and around the ring I imagine
you must have wheeled,
as the mustached trainer, nervously

cropping his thigh, barked pointers from center ring,
my mother seeming to float above her cut-back saddle
as you racked on.

I'd heard of the ribbons
you sported before the war.
Before your trainer was called to the North Sea

and the groom to the South Pacific. Before my mother,
ambushed by marriage and childbirth, left, too,
then returned to the house of her childhood.

Fifty years of opening the same windows
to the usual shadows and drafts.
Daylight struck over and over.

I'd ride over you,
coaxing my pony down the hillside
that cradled your secret of bones.

Impatient in your dark nest,
you'd kick inside the earth, the hillside shimmering.
Though you were not so much

as an indentation,
the goldenrod coloring the hillside
late summer, your temperamental monument.

Still, I was told you were there,
Noble Knight, Solid Mahogany, Emerald Future.
The hillside was a mirror

in my mother's life, and then in my own.
We opened our eyes to see into it.
All my young life, I believed you were there.

I'd canter bareback dodging brush and limbs
down the hillside graves to the Sugar Bush
where Grandfather's sapping shed sank

plank by rotting plank to the earth
and the maple trees grew huge and unwieldy, left long
      untapped.
The body-stench of crude oil rose from pockets

in the Pennsylvania marsh,
and the trails that I pretended wound forever
ended. I sensed you were there.

We are repeated
on the backs of saddled ponies—
my mother, my children, and I

(car-bound, fiddling with my keys)—
a young woman revised
in the clunky staccato of small hooves

wearing circles in a ring,
each circuit ending
and ending again.

Notes, 1973

She bends over a gleaming keyboard,
cup of coffee cooling on the music rack.
She has been here for decades, with her
Couperin and Rameau,
while I slip back and forth, searching
for what will marry me
to something so dear.
It's all right to sift through
without greater purpose or goal,
though blankness mars a girl's day:
round as a pie, with pieces cut
into delicious triangles
I learn to savor
from my mother,
who in turn, teased it from hers.
I stay busy, productive,
check off the day's list
as if it is about to burst into flame,
to stir nighttime embers
in exchange for jobs well done.
I am brushing my teeth, I am plunging the brush
into the way back, polishing my to-do's,
as Alberti winds his way
down the cobblestone street
from his century, to mine.

This Church

My daughter cried when we left the cathedral at Chartres.
All over France, I carried her out of churches
as she clung to me inconsolable, pointing back
into the vaulted dark, and sobbing.

I, too, was awed by the light
that sifted through stories
in the stained glass; was held snug
in the cool dark belly of the nave
as it swallowed our hushed, echoey voices,
returning them to us as the whispers
of many. Two among hundreds, we filed

past icons and altars with their tiers
of votive candles, past the worn tombs of sleeping martyrs.
Not wanting to disturb the faithful few
praying from the rows of hard-backed chairs,
I slipped silently from chapel to chapel,
my toddler, lagging a little behind.
I lit a candle for Caitlin,
one among so many lives here burning

for those who've felt cool water on the forehead
and tasted the body, bland until it's dipped in blood;
perhaps judged the cassocked men

who drained the cup too quickly after mass;
or those who asked too many questions
as they trembled their way with or without God
down the cramped aisles of churches
where they were baptized and confirmed and married to men
who would help return to them the mystery of a child
who cried when she was forced to leave
the cathedral at Chartres.

Old Love

My daughter looks up at me
through ghost light,
her frayed pointe shoes glowing
from the wall above her bed.
She misses the old house.
I blink back, heartless with repetition—
Sleep, you've got to sleep,
I say again, *it's late.*

She'll cry wolf throughout her adolescence
as things around her slide from proper nouns
to adjectives—the ancient cat, Celine,
we've fed for fifteen years
is Old Cat now; the babysitter mare,
Nothin' Easy, so long in the tooth we forget
how old exactly, is Old Mare;
and the house we sold and left,
is the Old House,
where the old family lived, the one
with a father still in it.

As if things most precious to us
lose their specificity with age or distance.
As if they're tropes
for our own failing hearts, preparing

for what's about to be lost,
or is already—the way a stray cat
beelined to our Baltimore row house doorstep
and in a blink of years I felt her life
dissolve in my arms. Or the house
we brought the newborns to one February,
one May, when the snow rolled down its velvet
carpet, and the peonies were in bloom
and it was still 15201 Wheeler Lane
and we were not yet broken enough by nostalgia
to never want to go back after the midnight
of our marriage, even for one sleepless moment,
to the time we were young
and still surprised by the world around us,
and everything was new and nothing
did we call, even lovingly yet,
Old Cat, Old Mare, Old Love.

Once a Month He Gets the Kids

All morning I parsed the walls
of the closet apartment, listened to you worry
the children over a few spilled crumbs,
smudges on a tabletop.
I couldn't breathe.

Now the land speeds by
as if on a mission.
Through the train window,
cities flickering like stray thoughts, the miles
unreeling homeward, and I thought
of what cleaved us—what we'd given up
and gotten. Maybe we should
rejoice. All night from my farmhouse window
left ajar, I, too, become the rusty song
of sliding barn door hinges.

Burning the Barn

Caitlin rounds the corner of the bank barn.
I reach behind my back to hide my cigarette
as I stub it out—I don't want her to see
the thing in me he hated.

I slide open the warped red door
just in time to join a samba with fire
wreathing the barn floor. I kick and cover,
while Barrett hauls a hose
from the house.

Caitlin calls the fire department,
and the whole neighborhood comes running
to meet the new owner of the farm
whose only recourse is to admit
what she's done, and that she's a smoker—
that, after too many years

of burning barns,
she'd left a husband, and still
doesn't know how to tell the truth
to her daughter,
or to flick a cherry out.

God Bless the Bid

We offer some platitudes
about trying her best,
while Caitlin sits in the backseat,
fidgeting tights over toes,
folding extra fabric under a foot.
You crank the heat up to "high."
I want to talk about the horse
I'd let escape from the field.
I want to admit how I'd hated that horse
who'd try to dig his way out when kept in,
slip through the gate when turned out,
who'd kicked my own horse's bad knee.
To help kill what you think you hate
then to live without it and want it back, I want
to talk about that—
how easy it was to slip on the ice
to let the gate swing open
and let the horse get away.
Our years together now speaking
through Caitlin's curling toes.
Then through twenty other daughters
cramped in the overheated car,
lining up at the barre, seeking
perfection in the lift
of an elbow, the flex of a toe.

And our own, just one among many
craving to be special, to catch the right eye,
to have the gate swing open
just for her. Our silence is her
slender growing body
straining to follow the other girls' feet.
It is the fog of headlights, the strange look
in the horse's eye
as I held him by the side of the road,
singing *Blacks and bays, dapples and greys,*
and all the pretty little horses
just before he went down.

The Museum of Modern Art at 6:00 am

It's a Degas in the shower,
Caitlin bending from the waist,
one leg propped on the tile,
her skin dolphin-slick
with shaving cream and shampoo,
breasts and sex obscured
by textured glass.

She's got tendonitis now, can't dance
when dancing is the passion.
I bring her *Wuthering Heights*, chewing gum,
new reins for her pony's bridle,
confide a few of my own blues.
Because I'm no dancer and cannot comprehend
the meaning of sore ankles,
she asks me to knock
before entering her room,
greets me by turning away.

Without knowing it, she gives me a gift
as she does her ankle exercises
to Joni Mitchell before dinner
and Cass Elliott after.
Voices infiltrate our house,
as do the dancers in their hushed pinks

stretching and bending
from the poster on her wall.
Each wincing moment a foreboding
of what they want most, yet won't be able to have.

Notes, 1986

I am as old as I've ever been.
It seems I will go on,

having known great pain,
yet free of pain. Holding

what is separate from me
yet a part of me, too.

Looking down with vast longing,
yet separate.

A garden behind us,
a white picket fence.

Soldiers of corn, tomatoes, and peas.
Her face unchartered, yet wise.

To think I might go on
with an infant, a fence, a gunmetal sky—

me gazing down
at the face of the future, while she stares

at the mechanical eye, already
yearning for something not-me.

The Get-A-Way

2:00 am

My daughter dashes into my room to wake me—
a fire alarm blares from another cottage.
She's wearing her clogs, clutching
her frayed blanket—her most prized possessions,
she tells me later
when all is safe. She can't rouse
her brother or me—him, the adolescent slug;
me, the divorcee, who's had too much to drink.
If I'm going to die, then let me die on vacation.
And so she's out the door
to save herself, at least.

6:00 am

The yellow-breasted bird
calls for more pretzel crumbs
I'd left him on the balcony; the swish
of a coconut palm outside my window
and the waves along the shore
repeating their old refrain, reassure me
that nothing's wrong. Beyond all this,
through Drake's Channel, an O'Day Mariner
lazes by the deep-within-me

where the glasses of wine I drank for dinner
have long since finished their mean lull-a-bye.
I pull the cool white sheet over my head.
Let me burn.

Why I Love to Drink

Driving through a suddenness
of March snow, listening to a radio talk show

about parents who let their children
drink at home, I winced. Kept driving,

loving the snow, the feel
of the road in the snow.

I grew up drinking because my parents drank.
Wine with dinner, Mother insisted,

pouring her fourth, turning her cheek
the other way if I mixed a little rum

with my juice, said nothing about
my sloe gin and cranberry mixers

behind the football field.
They pretended not to know, hoped

if problems weren't addressed
they would just go away. Over time,

my compulsion to tell the truth
became as strong as my compulsion to conceal.

Not a day goes by I don't at least think
about having a drink

as others long for their children.
My mouth waters as I glance at my watch

craving after a long day the first cool sip
of Anapamu, the color of figs, the first

dialed-up sensation as the smoothness
glides down the chute of my throat.

My daughter looks away,
my son wants a sip.

For a few sweet moments
until the duller repetitions

of the second drink set in—
loving the snow, the feel

of the road in the snow—
I am swallowing the world.

The Shower Cap

I unfold the musty-sweet of Grandmother's Lake Chautauqua.
Churning in the bathroom mirror in my first striped two-piece,

I was all alone with her lily-scented soaps and porcelain swans
      and shower cap,
as sailboats lazed on the water outside her very pink window.

It was a plastic cap, with little colored dots
scattered over the hood and a terribly frayed elastic,

which, in all the world, could only have been hers.
Though my mother hated her own mother,

she chose the signature keepsake,
then left it at the bottom of a dresser drawer for twenty years.

Each Easter, without fail, the pot of lilies would arrive
in a delivery truck chugging up the drive.

I never had to check the card to know the sender.
No longer. These things I can never own

but only choose and guard and then pass on—
grandmother's shower cap,

and the pervasive scent of Mother's lilies,
tucked between the lines of this poem.

Blue Stuff

Half-past Chardonnay before I noticed
the swimming-pool blue of the aquarium,
among the tetras and sucker fish and angels
treading the drugged water,
two dollops lying unfocussed on the gravel floor.
I made a mental note
to start here in the morning,

when two more were dead.
I spatula-ed those silver eggs
down the toilet, planning
to tell the children when they'd
gotten home from school, the navy water,
Van Gogh's starry sea.

In an idle moment between piano
and TV, John discovered all the rest
bobbing on the surface.
Except one fat angel who'd made it through
two other Armageddons of this aquarium tank.
A lot of commotion,
scooping and splashing, phoning
a long-distance father
who'd surely add this to his list
of my failures.

Caitlin stood silently by, wide-eyed,
counting cupfuls of the blue stuff
she'd tossed in without asking,
only trying to be helpful.

I pulled her close
to explain the difference
between intent and accident,
and simply having too much to do.
Admitting that I too have put too much blue stuff in,
only to watch what rises, bellies up,
or clings to the thermometer.
Remembering how I'd turned my own burning cheek
one too many times the other way,
the fragments of our family
floating still life in the sky
above Saint-Remy-de-Provence.

The Art Project

She hauled it home
in her brother's VW,
scratched the hatch paint
when she pried it out,

carted it up stone steps
and into the mud room.
"We had to show movement
and light," she informed us.

"Everyone else made kaleidoscopes,
but I had my heart set on a chair."
She hammered for hours in her art class
the seat of the old metal stool

where she spied
splintered versions of herself.
"Art as a wound," we joked
around the dinner table,

"downright dangerous at that,"
wincing at the shards
of mirror glued on top
of our dented images, concertina wire

wound around the stainless legs,
until we imagined a two-step forming,
debutante in her stiff
hoop skirt swooping

over a gleaming floor
balanced on the arm
of some tantalizing stranger,
becoming our daughter's future

she crafted
with wire and broken glass.
We keep it in the garden,
daring us to sit, or dance, or look

more closely at the painful puzzle
    of ourselves
amid the columbine and daisies

and an old leather shoe.

Something With Diamonds In It

I'm looking out my family-room window
        when I see a man I don't know,
bare-chested, barefoot, and towel around his loins,
        scooting out the back door.

Coffee cup in hand,
        I blink and look again.
From inside, my daughter's turned the knob,
        looking furtive over a shoulder, as if for me.

Caitlin's back from six weeks in The City
        interning for Avenue Q and preferring
a father who now speaks Manhattan.
        Next, two more boys

race out the front door toward their jalopies.
        Scanning the driveway,
I count twelve more cars.
        I'm as ashamed as I am miffed.

Should I punish
        or choose something with diamonds in it,
the glitter of kindness?
        What's her secret?—

questions I no more know how to answer
        than I know how to end this
one-night stand under the lonely sky,

except to wrap a towel around
        and scoot it out the back door
with all the blushing others.

Notes, 1990

Easy, to take another lover to your bed
and to let him ease into someone else's,
when you are loath to love yourself.
Bishops and Queens scrambling undressed
to their respective squares: a Budapest Gambit
when you have a pawn's self-esteem.
I thought love could be bought
or traded, that I better dress up
like a working girl, or be left
on the board, victory as failure,
our water cooler, burbling
untouched in the corner.
My daughter has taken her time.
She is not afraid of being alone
with the self, who offers
darkness when tired,
and when thirsty, a paper cone of water.

Cream of Tartar

Pot-holdering a cloud
of baked soufflé,
its voluptuous body
billowing over the dish,
we kept its infallible, flawless mystery,

referencing the butter-
stained recipe card
by memory only.
Teamwork—we'd wink to each other—
and lots of stirring, never revealing

what separated mother and daughter
from our guests' amazement
at this seeming perfection—
fleeting, and only as good
as our shortcut:

a bitter white powder lodged
in a glass bottle,
that doubles in volume without fail
what it starts with, transforming
impossible into easy.

Mateus

Anything made with that much butter
has got to be good.
Also, chestnuts
roasting on a barrel fire

after an evening church service,
a Bach Chorale and Kyrie
the choir sang
in a meandering key.

The cheese wafers passed
on a hubcap tray
from grown-up to grown-up,
and finally, to me.

We'd already opened our mouths
for the body of Christ,
then popped and peeled
and stuffed and swigged—

not sherry, not Chardonnay,
not rose, nor rum.
So thick and sweet,
what was it—

glass after glass
staunched by the butter and guilt
of Mother's offering?
Enamored of the new

church organist, she barely glanced
beyond her crescent-moon of guests
at her adolescent daughter,
learning to be transfigured,

then lost.
When I'm fifty,
I want to gyrate to death, she teased,
with a certain vanity that made her locally famous.

She'd read about someone who did it
in the *Sunday Styles*.
How many seasons would she have left?
I sat counting with a half-empty glass

in my small cupped hand.
I was the pinch of salt,
Mother, the tablespoons of butter.
Allan the organist,

the smirking cupful of cheddar.
I was learning my lessons well.

Not Malbec, not Merlot, nor Montepulciano.
If I leave it,

maybe it will come back to me,
the way, sometimes, the only way
to see your daughter
is to turn away from her.

Whatever it was,
I became hooked on the daily Mass of drinking.
Though I could never again eat chestnuts,
and I'd replace that cloying wine

with Chardonnay by the battleship,
I still tipple from that night—
I believe it comes in a squat glass bottle
and is the color of a girl's first blood.

Summoned

We'd sit with hands folded on laps
in her slip-covered chairs,

mouths watering for hard sauce, gravy,
croque messieurs and dessert meringues.

Grandmother's swollen feet
stuffed into satin flats with toddler bows

stabbing under the table
for the elusive buzzer.

We cringed at what the harsh noise brought—
a person to attend to all our needs.

Nanny would complain that the chicken
was never hot enough, Bette

never fast enough, and deaf as well.
Hotter if I'd gone to get it myself,

we'd mimic in the station wagon's back seat,
overfed and restless, heading home.

*

My grandmother died, followed closely
by Bette—my shiva interrupted by my daughter,

sick in bed upstairs,
bragging, when well enough to talk,

about the ten times she's already puked.
A scratchy intercom summons me

from the barn, the Bette-in-me offering
crushed ice, popsicles, and ginger ale,

grateful to the cat for keeping Caitlin
company in my stead.

I open the window on fraught spring air
and the goings-on in the old maple,

the roiling ocean of its lime-green leaves.
Sitting in my spurs and chaps,

I feel the frantic-in-me dying,
because my daughter wants

to share her aimless sense of sick time.
It's all right not to do a thing

but listen to the catbird in the tree,
rub her thigh and count to one hundred,

move from bed to stairs to door to barn
and back again, with the progress of a love,

which only goes away
so it can come right back.

Under the Influence

1.
The kitchen's too small—
Out-Schmidt, auf Wiedersehen
my chorus, as I sought

the privacy to pour a second
and third, without her young soul-windows
to scold me.

The cauldron bubbled,
awaiting its ingredients,
peppermint candle aglow,
six eggs perched precariously

on the blue tile counter's edge—
a new jug of Woodbridge
lying in wait in the larder.

Not enough room,
which is why
Caitlin never learned to cook.

2.
Closer to smirched than narcoleptic,
I'd soak in the bathtub,

after barbecued meatballs and my fifth.

She kept reappearing in the doorway,
Mom, are you awake?
Hasn't everyone heard of a mother
who drank and drowned in a tub?

I waited till she'd left for college
to curb the nightly excess.
Now it's a single glass brimming over
instead of the whole damn bottle.

I can't take anything back.

Atlas

Mother mapped an index card
matching each line to a grocery aisle—
she knew exactly where everything lived at Big Joe's.

I try to remember where the coffee is,
the light bulbs and Splenda, as I sit at my desk
shaking off a vodka sweat.

Scissors for the blooming peonies I place
close to Saskatchewan, Band-Aids for my cut finger
that won't heal, farther south toward Antigua.

I'm following in her pen-steps, although poorly:
mine can't match hers in my hasty cartography
which will mean a lot of back and forth

between hemispheres.
Her map allowed detours and blank spaces
for last-minute cravings, and elbow room,

browsing the shelves, sharing news
or recipes with neighbors.
Have you met the new church organist?

I was learning how to ask for things,

attach strings and visualize my goals.
Can I have a Bit-O-Honey, please?

Marking items on an index card
in order of their placement in the store,
leaving room for what I wouldn't need

for thirty years, following her recipes,
or longing for answers to questions
I never dared, or forgot to ask.

What to cover the turkey with—
tinfoil or cheesecloth?
How long to simmer garlic for al olio,

how to tell my daughter she needs a change of scenery.
Caitlin, if I stare long enough at the uncharted space,
will a new route to your Brooklyn appear?

Their Fantastic Mother

I cook for them to cover up
my not wanting to go on vacation,
to pick them up from school,
to help them memorize times tables

or capitals of Honduras and Peru.
They return for holidays
and occasional weekday overnights.
I joke that I'm a fantastic mother
and an exceptional cook,

like the good runner who doesn't like to run
but does it anyway
to relieve guilt through accomplishment.
They are always glad to see me—

Caitlin plopping duffels of laundry
in the mudroom; John
with a sitar case the new puppy
drags across the kitchen
as if it were a dead deer.

My son jogs downstairs smiling
as I pour my first Chardonnay,

inviting himself to join me. When I offer,
he asks, as if it were fifteen years ago,

Hey Ma, what's for dinner?
I say frog tamales and boiled puppies,
and he provides Rumi for a dinner prayer—
The lion is most handsome when looking for food.

Chocolate Sauce

I'm here to entice
you to sit down
at your abandoned
dining room table,
after the kids
have long gone,
their shipwrecked seats
still stained
with dried ketchup
and soy sauce.
Invite someone
over for dinner
you haven't seen
in a while. Begin
to set aside the time
with four things at hand—
chocolate, cream, sugar
and pinches of
any sweet something
you choose to add:
maybe that longed-for trip
to St. John,
or a new career,
maybe the words
I'm sorry or *I love you*—

essential ingredients
in anyone's cupboard.

Notes, 1995

"Ride into the violet," he whispers,
as I settle into the stirrups.
It will take me nearly thirty years
to figure out what he means.
I don't know that yet
as I lived this then,
distance and time lugging their backpacks
unsparingly—
I wanted horses, trees, a farm.
Though I already had you,
and yes, your brother, too.
"Ride into the violet,"
he says again about that place
where fear turns into courage.
I'm kicking my guts out decades later
galloping out.

From Finding My Distance

(2004)

Baden's Stream

Someone gets bucked off, a horse goes lame, we run into a hunt, a dog falls through ice. My horse slips on some early-morning dew. Caitlin stands over me. "Mom, wake up!"

We make our way through chunky footing, the kind that results after weeks of mud, a good freeze, and a better thaw. Caitlin, only reaching 5 foot 2 to my 5 foot 10, never grew out of her old pony. We come to Sunny's favorite stream, and punch through ice to wade across.

Maryland

Christmas has not made up for the restlessness Caitlin feels being near me again. I know this is normal, and yet my feelings get hurt. Today, a CD of hers is missing. She's sure that I've done something with it. I fail to remind her that I barely know how to work the CD player. Who are the Smashing Pumpkins, anyway?

The weather has decided to be fickle again. We trade long undies for short sleeves. I call over my shoulder, "Follow me!" and I take off, with my daughter on my tail, over the split rail, the coop, the table, and up the hill to the bank jump. Galloping away from the coop, I glance back at the girl, now in midair over a fence. She is smiling.

Wires

A phone call from New York. "Hey, Mom, would you like to come to The City next weekend for that show you got me tickets for?" I glance down at my calendar, paging to that day, which is already filled. I black out the World Horse Expo in Timonium. "You bet," I say, "Thought you'd never ask."

New York City

A blizzard forecast from Norfolk, Virginia to Portland, Maine: 12 to 24 inches of snow. Winds gusting to 50 miles per hour. Paralyzing windchill, existentialism. I am determined to make it to New York via Amtrak. The snow starts somewhere in Jersey. By the time I meet up with Caitlin in a coffee shop, a foot has already fallen. We dash next door to *A Number*, Caryl Churchill's play about cloning and a father's strained relationship with his original son and two of the clones.

We smear our way through the snowy streets. The blizzard continues through our early dinner at the Hudson Hotel and into the night, as Caitlin and I toss and turn on the scanty mattress in the art deco room that is no bigger than a foaling stall. Caitlin has asked to stay with me and I offer to share the tiny space with my insomniac daughter. She will have to read and watch TV till 3:00 A.M. When she finally falls asleep, she talks and carries on with the imaginary characters in her dreams, as she has done since she was little.

Caitlin loves The City.

A blizzard fifteen stories up—there's a kind of beauty in it. I try not to let my daughter see how my mind has wandered back to Maryland. My heart is kicking drifts away from the barn door.

Nowhere

Caitlin boycotts nightly telephone calls. An effort to work things out herself and not to rely on me for answers to the endless questions of her life. I feel as though I weigh one thousand pounds, as if I were a horse who's gotten into the feed bin and can't stop eating until I colic on the profound heaviness of Caitlin's absence.

Maryland

We are still having 20-degree nights and the mercury is not reaching much past 45 or 50 during the day. We're all sick of it.

I take my daughter a rainy 40 miles away to meet a school friend whom she will hitch a ride with to Sarah Lawrence. She doesn't want to go back to school, which I take as a compliment. It has been so nice to have her home. Hello, spring and solitude and having the house to myself again. But goodbye, little girl and big girl Caitlin. It's a tough trade.

The Glass Menagerie

I'm a big fan of Jessica Lange. She is vibrant and appropriately strained in the role of the fading southern belle and jilted wife and mother, Amanda. But I am distracted by extraneous hand and arm movements of the actors. Even Jessica gets a bit carried away. In the cinema, there are a lot of partial shots in the filming of a scene but on stage we get the whole actor—no subtractions—who must act with her entire body and can't hide a thing.

And what to do with the hands? The hands in the process become as constant and evident as facial gestures. Christian Slater, in the role of the unhappy dreamer son, Tom, seems comfortable on stage, perhaps because the director has given him something to do with his hands at all times: smoking. Ms. Lange puts her hands to her heart a lot which is a poignant gesture for this unhappy, hysterical belle, but she's less effective when her arms go flying about in more awkward, pained moments. I think of myself, pushing and pulling my horses around tough tracks, way too noisy and distracting with my hands. The best art is when there's a lot going on but it doesn't look like it. The sleight of hand, the quiet ride, the ballerina seemingly effortless in her difficult leaps and arabesques.

Saturday. Get as close to Caitlin as I can.

I kiss Caitlin goodbye. As I wait for a cab, I watch her back and unpulled mane of dark, wild hair recede down the bustling Sunday streets and still-brilliant skies of the Upper East Side on her way back to Grand Central and back to school. My chest constricts, something rises within it, and I want to reach out and pluck her back, my own camera's eye swelling and burning.

Arizona

Dear Caitlin,

When I'd moved to Arizona for my first teaching job, I was unhappy and lonely. I missed home and my first big love who had moved to Mexico with his saxophone. Your grandmother made a suggestion: Why not join the church choir? It was a logical thought coming from my mother—she was a good Episcopalian and an even better musician. But for me? We all know what my voice sounds like. I joined St. Barnabas Choir in Phoenix.

So, does Sarah Lawrence have a choir?

Wires

The wisteria tree is in full bloom. News from my daughter of a summer job offer in a bakery in SoHo and a sublet in Tudor City. It's not my idea of summer fun, staying in hot, stinky New York City frosting cupcakes, but she sounds bright and happy. Definitely on the upswing.

Another call. Yet another audition rejection. If she loves what she does, she should keep doing it, I say. The process matters most, I say.

"Oh my God, Mom," she asks, panic in her voice, "you aren't writing down this conversation, are you?"

Maryland

I head up to the barn for my first of many re-inspections of Ballerina's huge, waxy udder. I struggle to stay awake until Caitlin's arrival around eleven, armed with day-old cupcakes. I listen with detachment to her tales of The City and the life she has chosen over this one. I crave the undulations of my mattress and I'm already making lists in my head of tomorrow's activities with the horses. Caitlin now lives in the next field over with the other yearlings, having grown huge with a life of her own.

New York City

I take the train up to New York to spend the night, get a feel for the sublet and a tour of Magnolia Bakery.

My claustrophobic tendency is exacerbated by The City with its crowds and smells and expanses of buildings and blocks. Caitlin is unfazed by the dirt and the noise and the heat, is thrilled to be able to show off her comfort level with her new knowledge of New York. I try to seem enthusiastic about the warm sushi at lunch, the miles of walking in flip-flops on hot, dirty streets, the broken air-conditioning in the dress shop. We sweat through the expensive, ill-fitting dresses we try on. I talk to Caitlin about what's going on at home but there's a new distance that has opened up between us. Her heart is in New York and mine is in Maryland. I am eager to leave The City but reluctant to leave my daughter. This inner conflict produces a splitting headache and a slight queasiness for my twenty-four-hour visit. I want to slip her in my pocket and take her away.

Maryland

It takes three hours to make an hour-and-a-half trip from Seneca, Maryland to the train station, thanks to three bumper-to-bumpers, including a bad accident that involves a tarp draped over a wrecked VW Bug and the closing of I-70 in the opposite direction, with cars crossing over the median strip and heading the wrong way on the deserted interstate to escape the 5-mile-long jam on my side. The cops are too busy with the accident to worry about impatient motorists' infractions. Just as the traffic starts moving, I get stuck in Orioles' baseball traffic. I finally arrive at the train station, frazzled and more than an hour late to pick up Caitlin, who's tapping her toes on the curb when I pull up, with a gigantic smile on her face.

Nowhere

Caitlin started her movie internship today. Maybe she won't come home for that weeklong visit after all. The movie people need as much of her as they can get. Ballerina is grazing in one corner of the paddock and letting Selery Salt gallop over to the fence to say goodnight to me. I give his star and snip a pat, rub his forehead and then his butt, and he leans into my rubbing the way the babies always do.

Maryland

Caitlin calls from The City: "I'm about to get on a train home."

"Today?"

Baden's Stream

The horses know the way, and we feel their excitement on the last part of the mucky trail before the stream. They plunge down the rocky slope and into the water, making a beeline for the deepest spot, to stand, for as long as we'll let them, with the canopy of trees over us and Daisy and Simon swimming circles in slow motion around us.

Caitlin takes issue with all of us having to drive together to a Fourth of July party. Our ground fireworks blossom into sky-works as the argument progresses to sensitive issues like money and her chosen summer path in New York. I press her buttons and she presses back, and by the time we pick up her brother at his summer digs, we're screaming at each other. Barrett sits silently in the rear seat like Ben Franklin, having given up any hope of productive diplomacy. Caitlin doesn't want me in the car anymore, so John and I end up driving separately to the party.

Both Caitlin and I are pretty good social actresses and at the party, you'd hardly guess we'd had a problem. I don't think she has any more fun than I do but we laugh and joke with other guests and talk as if life were hunky-dory. An hour or so later, after John has already joined his friends, Caitlin and Barrett and I make a hasty retreat, long before the fireworks at the Inner Harbor even begin. We stop off at a sushi place and pig out on nigiri and rolls. It's as if nothing has happened between us, and we're pleasant over dinner. The three of us are exhausted from our day and decide that bed is the best place to be. We fight lines of traffic at Oregon Ridge, hatchbacks and sedans and trucks on their way to northern Baltimore County's blooming skies: cars stacked up along the sides of the back road we duck onto off the main clogged drag, children and coolers perched on roofs, families lugging blankets and chairs to get a little closer to the magic. "Fireworks are so fucking dumb," Caitlin says.

"I wish you wouldn't use that word so much," I say.

"Which one?" she asks. "You mean *fireworks*?"

We negotiate this long, unhappy day and return home. It's upstairs for me for a long soak in the tub and bed. "If I open the window, do you think we could hear them?" I ask my drowsy husband. Without waiting for an answer, I crack the window, and sure enough, I hear distant thunder. I imagine what we missed, blossoming over the water at the Inner Harbor. I think of the hordes of people, heads tilted up, arms around each other, waiting expectantly. I see them against the black sky of my closed eyes, big and full and startling with a kaleidoscope of colors.

New York City

It takes forty-five minutes to make it the short twenty blocks through noon-hour traffic to my daughter's sublet on the East Side. I'm worried about having left the farm so soon after Ballerina's death.

~

Caitlin's idea of showing me a good time is to comb the hot streets in search of food. I put on my walking shoes and we trek for miles, taking small breaks from pavement trotting to ride the subway. The restaurants are on par with the subterranean tram: hot, cramped, dark, and noisy. I can't get the last few days out of my mind. But I'll bite my tongue a thousand times for the sake of my daughter who wants to eat and eat. Though she's only nineteen, she orders a mojito at dinner. "I'm the D.B.," she says, "the director's bitch. I bring coffee to Zach Braff."

~

I yearn for the quiet of the farm. Sirens squeal sixteen stories below. Our second night is Sushi Samba, a Japanese/Brazilian fusion place with a loud fever beat. After a platter of Ipanema handrolls, Caitlin wants to go to a Russian bar. We take a herky-jerky cab ride to the Lower West Side and down some steps into Gluttony. We order pear martinis. I don't hesitate to blink at her request. She loves putting on her sophisticated demeanor when she talks to the waiters, as if she's been ordering martinis since the day she stopped wearing diapers. Down our sleepy, already-buzzed gullets go the pear martinis, which assures that my headache will increase and expand well into tomorrow.

~

Caitlin asks how her pony Sunny is doing. "He's okay," I say, "but he's still quite off." Caitlin has grown accustomed to our care of Sunny in her absence, as well as reports of his intermittent lameness.

"So what's wrong with him?" she asks.

"He's got old pony disease," I say.

Caitlin admits she doesn't want me to go. The streets are the quietest they've been since my arrival. I get teary as she locks up her sublet and we head out to find a cab. I hug her hard and climb in for another chrome-yellow roller-coaster ride to the train station.

Wires

Caitlin calls in a whisper. She's still on set and can't talk, yet she's dying to be calling me from a movie set. "Gotta go," she says.

Maryland

We sit down to crabs and Caesar potato salad, corn on the cob and tomatoes from our garden. We pound and pick. This will be the last time we sit down together for a while, as Caitlin returns to New York tomorrow. John's friend, Andy, with whom he backpacked through Europe, stops by after we are stuffed and the newspaper tablecloth, with its heaps of shells and pickings, has been crumpled and tossed. He shows us pictures of their trip on his laptop. We see goofy close-ups of John and his gang, we see the Senegalese friends they made and pictures of the wrapped joints they legally bought and smoked. "They even came with bar codes," Andy pipes up. We see the

Crooked Lady in her official package followed by a shot of John stoned and lost in a haze of smoke in a neon pink hostel.

Wires

"I'm in the hospital with my second A.D. Didn't Barrett tell you?" Caitlin says, breathlessly. I'm thrown into a panic. *When did she ever have her first A.D.?* "Yeah, she fell in a hole. She stepped off a curb in Times Square and there was this big hole in the street she fell right into." The Hollywood lingo comes back to me: assistant director, first assistant director, second assistant director, then intern. "I told her that in all my years of riding, I'd never seen a worse fall. We're waiting for x-rays. They think she may have broken her wrists. I'm helping her," she adds.

Maryland

My ex-husband and his wife unexpectedly swing by the farm on the last leg of a summer's cross-country road trip. John arrives home road-weary from his return from Ithaca and his girlfriend, Mollie, about two seconds before our surprise company pulls up. I invite them to stay with us, then spend part of the afternoon engaging in awkward chit-chat. My ex pets Simon, then asks where the bathroom is so that he might wash his hands. They spend the late afternoon playing pool with John and then head out for a dinner of crabs. I know that John feels guilty for not having visited his father and stepmother earlier in the summer, and I want to help make this visit as easy as possible. That has always been my goal with my firstborn—to make things easy—and it is not always for the best. For some reason, I've let Caitlin struggle more than John, and she is stronger for it.

Our guests will return later, after we're asleep, to crash in Caitlin's room. The history of my younger life married to my first husband, before the farm and Barrett and my life with horses and older children, visits me in my dreams. I'm grateful to wake to Barrett beside me, sawing away.

Wires

Caitlin is having trouble with life at Sarah Lawrence and is thinking about transferring. She is missing out on the traditional college experience. She wants to go to a school that offers football and sororities. I could easily see Caitlin in that other environment but I also feel that it's not a matter of environment at all.

Maryland

I finish my barn work around six, in time for a quick bite before Barrett and I pick up Caitlin at the train station. She is bubbly and bossy when we greet her. I have done everything wrong in her absence: my hair is an awful color, the new shades in the upstairs hallway are tacky, and I look downright anorexic. I take a deep breath, knowing that brassiness and faultfinding are her ways of giving me a quick pat and showing how glad she is to see me.

Now we can nest. I hope I can turn away from my own sad blood muscle and horses and tune into Caitlin. My daughter wants to bake bread this rainy afternoon—nothing like baking bread to take away the blues. We try our mutual hands and elbows at sourdough biscuits. Dig, dig, dig we go. Pound, pound, pound. Rub it around until it feels just right. Get the old fingers working. Knead until they ache. Roll it out as thin as it will go. Smell the musty aroma wafting up, the poignant sweet and sour scents commingling: this bread, my life, my daughter.

Notes, 2003

My world hidden
in the everywhere of fog.
When it lifts, as it will,
then I'll get up
to tally the ledger,
crosshatch the fifth on those
railroad tracks of time, to slide beads, days.
Not many left of them now.
Go softly. Ever so
softly. You can control
the tone but not the pace
of growing old.
You haven't had
a child of your own, and likely
never will. You
were all I ever wanted. Four marks
of the pencil, perfectly straight
and standing tall, while the fifth
gets to slash them all, top left
to bottom right. That's you.

Shared Custody

They wait on the platform,
not even holding hands.

Caitlin gazes south,
willing the train to appear.

Her brother peers solemnly
into the tracks' dark well.

Her sandaled toes, tapping
in December's cold,

a Sendak Wild Thing
on John's softly-faded hoodie.

We are waiting for the 4:35
to New York, Penn Station

while the Silver Crescent with sleepers
—such exhausted angels—

idles on the southbound platform,
bound for Bayou St. John.

I check the station clock,
check it again.

Commuters tuck the folded wings
of newspapers underarm,

the dead weight of briefcases
handcuffed to the other.

Oh, the well-worn boredom
of a mother and her young

waiting peckishly
for time and expectation to merge.

As the Cyclopean eye
comes into distant view,

I scold myself for my impatience,
one hand now on either child

to hold her back
and nudge him forward—

The Anorexic Teaches Her Children

the art of eating artichokes.
Leaf by leaf, dipped,

not in irresistible butter,
nor mayonnaise and vinegar,

but just plain salt.
This is the heart of the matter—

paring the choke's
tiny fronds, exposing

the velvet disk. Time taken
to slice into wedges—

Ah, dense flavor!
Potent concentration!

I never want it to end—
more calories spent

than swallowed.
And the reward—

a discarded mountain
of shimmering leaves,

ending with more
than what I started with.

Southpaw

"Everyone has a plan until they get punched in the mouth."
—Mike Tyson

The right hand owns the melody
and time is on my side
as clock hands move.
Even the sun is synced with me
as it crosses my northern sky.
Watches, school desks,
scissors, baseball mitts, belts, books,
the chin rests of violins—a list
only a lefty can appreciate.
Though a southpaw's mother
gains some insight.
She bumps me with her left elbow
at supper, as I bump
her back with my right;
complaints from teachers
about upside-down cursive,
showing her how to braid
(over, under—or is it
the other way around?)
I can't teach
what I haven't learned.
With us at sixes and sevens

all through her teens,
she turns widdershins
to everything, though
the globe does move her way.
The Earth revolves left!
She's got me there.
But when I expect
to be needed—job application
rejected, lover gone AWOL—
I remain her main opponent.

      Blame's left hook out of nowhere knocks me out.

Ripple Effect

Water is a fickle muscle, teasing
the ball out, rippling it back toward shore
as faithful Georgia swims to fetch it.

I have been both water and dog,
panting for a man who loved me.
I have been hungered for

and left hungry like a lake
drained of its want.
I love you, I pleaded to Howie.

He moved to Mexico.
I love you, to Larry,
but he moved back home.

I love you, I lied.
Gary chose someone more truthful.
I hoped for better for my daughter,

but she loved and was left, was loved
and was gone, like fading sunlight
dancing on pond water.

"Someone will find me, won't they?" she asks.

Of course, I want to say,

but they'll have to swim for you.

Kites

I know only a little
about letting things go,

trying to contain them,
moving my gaze

just enough
to control drag and tension.

My daughter, for instance.

The closer,
the easier to manipulate.

The farther out,
more risk and thrill.

My fingers tease
the delicate rein—

now taut,
now giving.

The feeling,
the connection.

A westerly current
pulls me with it,

until a wind gust spins the parafoil kite,
plummeting earthward—

Notes, 2010

The daughter pushes once.
The self wavers, rights itself.
The daughter pushes again
and the "I" topples.
Pronouns melt in spring thaw.
Nouns scatter in a random wind.
Riddles of our childhood reignite,
the ones that rhyme.
The ones with all heart, no plan.
The sailor went to the sea sea sea
To see what he could see see see.
Pull and fetch, the I
  stands up straight like a wooden soldier,
and sleeps a little later each day.
Until verb rouses noun.
"Get up, get going! It's 10 of 7."
Ashes, ashes, we all fall down.
Already, sun has touched horizon,
phonics are starting to flee.
Noun stretches, yawns, rolls over
into space left by daughter gone
to bake a cake as fast as she can.
Raindrops greet morning.
No time to dream
about those childless university days

when all I had to do was think.

The Jockey

She wore a black skull cap
with red and white diamonds
stitched on the cover

and a pair of goggles
hitched up on the hard hat.
Her personal flare: a yellow whip
that Desormeaux had once tossed to her

and the medical armband she strapped
to her boot calf.
My arm is too small for it, she'd explain.
Eyes up, heels down.

Here it comes
welling up and spilling over.
Not pride, not regret, not sadness even.
But guileless determination

and the racing of years—
eyes up to the green light,
high heels clacking on sweltering pavement
as if a pony had just trotted by.

She sprints away from the market
with an armful of flowers, old dirt
flying up in her face
blurring the ticks between

the Start and the Quarter Pole,
his knock at the apartment door,
and her tiny urban kitchen
smelling of stir-fry and nasturtiums.

It Came to Nothing

all those horseshoes hammered
upright, umbrellas closed
in their stands, ladders
walked around,
4-leaf clover in a pocket,
a rabbit's foot nestling in another.
I'm still watching
the ole' pot that won't boil,
knocking on wood
to ward off misfortune.
I promise I've crossed
my fingers one too many times
for all those small lies
throwing a pinch of salt
over my shoulder
when I'd been clumsy in her kitchen.
I confess, I got it from my mother,
and she, from hers,
who also panicked in the presence of coal
cats. What did we possibly think
we'd be shielded from?
I still walk up the stairs backwards
on the last day of the month.
I hold my breath
when I reposition mirrors,

and never, ever, step on a sidewalk's crack.
And if bad luck comes in threes—
mother, daughter, granddaughter—
then nothing will save me
from not passing this on to you.

Birthday Gift

I consider an orchid,
long-lived and sensual,
but conclude its dormancy
requires too much patience.
Maybe something forever green
with nothing blooming,
like fiddle leaf or sansevieria.
The horticultural therapy program at NYU
advises, *Buy something that likes to live*
the way you do. Dark and smoky like her men?
Then prayer plants or dracaena.
Is it sunshine she craves?
Yucca, jade, or ponytail palm
placed in the eastern-facing window
she doesn't have.
Is she a well-meaning
over-waterer? Probably not.
Too forgetful, like me.
Then peace lilies or Chinese evergreen.
If a set-and-forget type—
a ZZ plant or philodendron
might be more her speed.
Too many thorns and doubts,
too much living done separately
to know my daughter well enough

to gift a plant.
They tell me I can't go wrong
with devil's ivy—
it can withstand pitch-black
and any level of moisture.
I push *Send*. At last her voice,
phoning at week's end—
Mom you got me devil's ivy
last year, and it died.

Nude Descending a Staircase

—after Marcel Duchamp, 1912

He'd be through college now—
big hands, dark eyes.
Maybe he'd scrimmaged
hoops in high school.

Or obsessed over luna
and cecropia moths,
among the largest
of their kind

and shortest lived—
having unformed mouths,
the gorgeous anorexics
cannot eat.

He might have had
his own family by now,
and gone sailing on weekends
where sand dollars are dark brown.

No matter.
Peter stays close, like a sea star
I pocket, miraculously unbroken.
"Hello," he greets me

from the bottom of the stairs
as I descend each morning,
robotic and calculated,
trailing broken versions

of my naked past behind me.
I'm no longer so young
for wonder not to become
regret, to love and miss

what I never had.

Owl

High up in the crown
of a Monterey cedar,
his saucer-yellow eyes
blinking down at us.
"Bird," says the wee'un.
"Owl," I specify.
Next morning, he's still
perched on the shaggy fronds,
a mouse in his talons, blood
stippling his feathers.
"Mouse," says the granddaughter.
"Breakfast," I elaborate.
I am not above revealing
cycles of violent need
to even the smallest person.
It will eventually make sense.
The girl will grow up
and learn to kill and kill and kill—
bugs, engines, books, time, love.
But for now, the owl stays high up in the tree top,
smugly at the center of his universe.
"Owl," says the budding girl.
"Life," says the old one, me.

Notes, 2014

My planet stopped spinning—
I'd listen at her closed door
for the faintest tone.
Nobody could hear me scream.

I suggested she leave it ajar.
There was a gulf of crisis
to close with worry, or love.
A gulf to close with forgiveness.
Ribbon of light under a door.

Ribbon of fear.
I talked to friends, counselors.
When she threatened to hurt herself,
I tried to talk to her. Oh that fierce, young,
wanting to be special. We survived,
she grew into her twenties, left those ribbons

behind. Traded them for rage
and a city filled with noise and rage.
Doesn't everyone need to be angry at someone?

Twenty-Six Point Two

(2014)

Maryland

My daughter is working on a one-woman, one-act play starring herself.

I worry that Caitlin is spreading herself too thin. I worry that she is too much like me. I worry that my horse is too much like all of us. I worry because, well, isn't that what I'm supposed to do? Lately, she has been writing plays. Still, she is vain about her proboscis, post sinus surgery, maybe in hopes of one day salvaging her career as a singer.

I expect her to arrive in a trench coat, hat, and shades, looking something like the Elephant Man, but she exits Penn Station all Brooklyn chic and unblemished—black pants, sweater, boots, coat, plus a black wool ski cap she has carefully positioned on her mop of wild long curly black hair. She is a huge, dynamic presence. Gorgeous, as always.

Our first stop is the grocery store. We comb our way through hundreds of ambivalent shoppers. Caitlin is accustomed to getting her way in crowds, and she's hardly polite about it. I push the buggy while she leads, twisting and bumping and dodging her way through the horde. I try to keep up with her, but it's hard work, without bashing into other shoppers. She complains that I'm slow, that I'm shopping impulsively as I pull items not on the list off the shelf, and that I can't keep up with her.

I return the chicken stock. I didn't mean to be impulsive.

New York City

Trains are either late, canceled, or sold out. My 10:04 is kyboshed. A control freak's worst nightmare. I buy a ticket for a later train and sneak onto the 9:30 which has been delayed till 10:00.

The ticket inspector frowns at my ticket and asks if I have any other paperwork. He mumbles something about needing to talk to the conductor, then leaves me alone for the rest of the trip.

If it's one degree it's a hundred in my coach car, and whether there's a malfunction, or we're all heating up the train with our communal anxiety to reach our daughters, is hard to say.

There's a track switch failure south of Philadelphia. We start moving again, only to wait in the station another half hour while a mechanic comes aboard to adjust the heat. I'd like to suggest we just open the windows and get going, but it's unlikely the window latches work either. Here comes my winter cold.

The taxi struggles in bumper-to-bumper traffic. I swoon with car sickness in the back seat.

Caitlin: *Are you here yet?*

Caitlin: *Where are you now?*

Caitlin: *Are you in a taxi?*

Caitlin: *What street sign do you see?*

The taxi lurches to a stop at a warehouse. I tiptoe up the slushy curb onto the sidewalk and open the grungy metal door. New York restaurants can't thrive unless they offer something distressed or un-New York—Mexican sushi, hand-frosted cupcakes, southwestern décor, or a restaurant that from the outside looks more like it manufactures steel than bruised kale omelets and superfood smoothies.

My twenty-eight-year-old daughter looks about fifteen in her pointy ski cap, black leggings, and pea coat. I'm glad she's drinking some exotic fruit juice concoction with wheat grass and asparagus, rather than a mimosa, which saves me from vouching for her age.

I request the lightest dish I can find on the menu—carrot and avocado salad with lentil soup—and pick at it for over an hour. Good old Caitlin, all 5'2", 100 pounds of her, orders an elk burger and tears into it.

"That's the great thing about running," she says. "I can eat anything I want."

In recent months, Caitlin has taken up jogging.

"I'm trying to qualify for the New York Marathon this year," she offers between jawfuls.

I casually praise her efforts while wondering how far this recent plan will go. I know nothing about human race running, though I do know a little something about conditioning for endurance and qualifying for an event. I know about the grit it takes to set sights on a nearly impossible goal.

Off to the spa for hoof treatments, and then—checking my watch—to the hotel for some fortifying grape juice. Then back onto frigid streets to make our reservation at Loco

Morandi. The maître d' presents us with some gooey-cheesy thing. We dive into it.

"What do you have in the way of Chardonnay by the glass?" I ask the frantic bartender across suits and ties and bejeweled fingers. He looks at me as if I've said a dirty word. I forget his name as soon as he utters it, which I never really hear anyway over the clatter and close, noisy quarters of the busy restaurant, full of boisterous gluttons, though it is already two hours before midnight.

"She's from Maryland," Caitlin explains to him.

The waiter tries to convince us to order several dishes and to share. I overreact with a resounding guffaw, elaborating how I absolutely do not like to share. Caitlin and I end up ordering the same dish, a salad that has so many ingredients I've no idea what I'm eating. I think fennel and something called Baquieu—handpicked by the three remaining virgins in Sicily—and who knows what else. Then a scallop dish. I need a periscope to find the seafood in among the greens. We're stuffed, and have to find room for the two dishes of on-the-house apple strudel that are brought to our table—two instead of one, I suppose, because of my earlier orneriness. Caitlin has no problem polishing off hers plus half of mine. Maybe I should take up running.

We hail a taxi. I ask if she'll visit Barrett while I'm in Aiken. I'm worried about leaving him so soon after his tuberculosis and hospital stay. She hesitantly says she will, but it feels like she's agreeing just to agree, with no intention of actually going through with the visit. Says she's crazy busy at work, is on deadline for a couple of grant applications, and has a race coming up. She wants to qualify for the marathon outright so that she won't be at the mercy of the lottery system. Maybe she's just plain too much like me: a woman with a program that only begrudgingly includes taking care of family. If she ever had a soft heart, living in New York has hardened it. Or maybe it's just that Caitlin has lived too long alone. I exit the taxi at the hotel, and Caitlin continues on to Brooklyn Heights.

Mission accomplished: I've wined and dined my daughter before my horse trip to South Carolina. At least Caitlin won't starve for the next few days. It feels too much like a duty done, though, rather than a connection made. I long to get lost in conversation with my daughter, to be engrossed in a subject, rather than always being slightly on the defensive.

I'm awakened by raucous goings-on in the room across the way. Various male voices laughing and shouting and one rich baritone breaking into the troubadour song from *Carmen*.

South Carolina

Barrett calls me from home.

"We just had shrimp for breakfast," Barrett tells me.

"We?" I say.

"Caitlin and I," he says.

Caitlin has gone home to check up on Barrett, after all. Good girl.

"She wolfed down an entire plate of shrimp benedict and then ate half of mine at Woodberry Kitchen. And her play was hysterical," he adds.

"Her play?"

A fight that started with her father in March is ongoing in April, the breakup with her boyfriend, same. Her unrewarding job of eight years still has its health-benefit hold on her.

I suggest she consider leaving New York, going somewhere where theater isn't so competitive.

"What, like Bawlty-more?" she asks, drawing out the syllables in her birth city's name, as if it were a dirty word.

"Well, maybe." It's true, I did notice that the local dinner theater is putting on a production of *Joseph and the Amazing Technicolor Dreamcoat*.

~

"Don't you ever check your emails?" I say. I've been forwarding Caitlin's emails to Barrett for a week because I couldn't bear to open them.

"Hardly," he says.

We sign off, and five minutes later he calls back.

"Caitlin is in *The NY Times*," he announces. "Her new play was voted one of the top new plays written by women."

"Where?" I say, "In Maryland?"

"In the country," he says. "For her play *When We Went Electronic.*"

I pull the rig over on the side of I-95, set the brake. The emergency lights flicker like two crickets. My daughter doesn't answer the phone.

Hopefulness is the sweet kiss of death.

The prospect of dining out is the first time all day I've seen Caitlin excited to do something. She raves about the Manor Tavern before we arrive, remembering the dinner we had there last summer with her boyfriend, who has recently dumped her for the second time.

"My husband will have the Mandarin chicken, and I'll have the canoe."

"It's quinoa, not *canoe*," Caitlin corrects me.

Caitlin drives us home. I'm exhausted, but my daughter is just revving up. She spends the next hour changing into a diaphanous lime-green swirly thing, and loading on more eye makeup, before she leaves for the tango festival—her chief reason for visiting.

At 4:30 a.m., the thudding of wheels on the drive. Barrett, just getting up to mop up the night sweats, goes downstairs to greet the stranger and make coffee.

From upstairs, I hear profuse apologizing.

"I'm really sorry, Barrett, I didn't know what to do."

I'm awake now. Barrett returns to our bedroom. "What was that all about?" I ask.

"Nothing," he reports.

~

Caitlin is sunbathing by the pool.

"Have you gone swimming yet?" I ask, innocently.

"The pool's disgusting. It's all green, and there's stuff floating at the bottom."

"It's just algae," I say. "We get it every year. You know, organic."

She pulls her sunhat down over her face.

I do some weeding around the pool.

"You really can't sit still, can you?" she accuses me again, muffled under her sun hat.

I ignore her, continue my satisfying work, yanking weeds, making things better. A white lily has multiplied and bloomed, its flowers so heavy they are toppling over, its perfume wafting my way.

~

"Mom, can you come here a minute?" Caitlin calls from the top of the stairway, having just gotten out of the shower, a towel wrapped around her tiny damp body.

"Is this really bad?" she asks, showing me her rosy cleavage, where the sun has made an impression. Her New York City skin is pale as china, and unaccustomed to wind, sun, rain, or snow. It is inside skin. Mine is outside. Hers definitely doesn't ride horses, pick stalls, weed gardens, or swim.

The scent of my mother's Easter lily follows me up the stairs to bed.

"I'm really upset about what I've done to my body," Caitlin says, entering the safe zone of my bedroom. She is deeply earnest about her irresponsible cleavage. And though she might never admit it, she needs to be close to me.

"It will be ok. It'll turn brown," I say, "and then it will be beautiful."

~

Caitlin is writing a play about a jockey who died in the starting gate at Santa Anita in 1971. Alvaro Pineda and his horse are the main characters. She and Barrett visit the Maryland Breeders' Association to do some research. When they pull back into the farm, I'm walking out of the mare barn, tacked up and ready to mount Patrick.

"Bring him here so I can pat him," Caitlin commands from the driver's seat, her tiny foot resting on the brake.

"Who's this?" I test her, holding Patrick, a dark bay with two white socks and a white umbrella on his forehead.

"Calvin," she says with assurance.

"Wrong," I say—the worst word I can utter to my daughter.

"Calvin doesn't have any white on him," I go on, like an idiot. She won't feel criticized, she'll feel invalidated, as if my asking her a horse question when she's been writing a play about horses is meant to undermine the integrity of her art.

Caitlin doesn't want to pick the remaining crabs from last night's dinner. She suggests that I buy already-picked jumbo lump from the store.

"Why would I do that, with all those uneaten crabs in the fridge?" I ask, bewildered.

"Because that's how we've always made them before."

Apparently, I don't pick them right and leave bits of shell. She then vanishes upstairs when it's time to make dinner.

She doesn't want to make crab cakes my way. She lists the ingredients she wants in them but leaves the scene before they're made. I turn to Oprah's recipe and bag the mayonnaise, hoping to satisfy my health-conscious daughter.

We sit down to dinner. Barrett saws into a dry crab cake.

"Who's this?" he says to Caitlin.

"Calvin," Caitlin replies. They both crack up.

A mountain of weeds encroaches on the house.

Wires

Caitlin writes scathing texts. I have never *supported* her, I love her brother more, I only *think* about myself, I am *painting* her in a corner. She will either *suffer* or *end* it. She never wants to *speak* to me again.

I call her other father.

"I'm in therapy myself. I can't sleep at night," Jack says.

I write back to Caitlin. I'm sorry she feels this way. I love her.

She says if I loved her I wouldn't *manipulate* her. I am why she feels like shit every day of her life. *Because, to you, I am never enough.*

My daughter. My beautiful, vibrant daughter.

~

Caitlin confesses that her boyfriend left her before her last visit home. Why does she always go for addicts? She answers her own question: because she feels worthless and unloved.

"Will anyone ever love me again?" she asks.

I say yes, you will love again, and be loved again and again, imagining the phantom children she will either have or not.

"Even my own father doesn't love me," she says.

"That's not true—he loves you," I say.

"He said he cared about his own life more than he cared about mine."

"That was just his therapist talking," I say.

New York City

I am on the streets of Brooklyn, my ex in his bowler hat, his wife beside him. We struggle to the tape that prevents us from going any farther. Thousands of spectators line the streets. I install the app to follow her progress, so we won't miss her. She and her father have made careful plans. When I complain of hunger pangs, Jack urges me toward the nearby bagel shop, while he and his wife position themselves at the appointed place, at mile 8. "How will I find you?" I ask, a bit nervously. I scan the masses around us; I've already gotten lost once in the New York Subway system, trying to follow Jack's directions. None of the taxis or buses are running. He motions downward, opening his leather coat; he is wearing a bright red, beautifully pressed Oxford—part of their plan.

"She's at mile 3," Jack says, frowning into his phone. "She's slow; I don't understand why she's so slow."

I vaguely recall Jack's own NYC Marathon run, maybe twenty years ago.

I take some shots of the little girls in the family next to us, their parents helping them hold out miniature hands so the first runners can low-five them.

"I think we may have missed her," Jack reports minutes later. "The tracker says she has already passed us."

We strain our eyes, the masses thickening in this first wave of the more elite runners. I get texts from John and Barrett. Everyone is tracking Caitlin's progress.

My tracker says she's almost at mile 6, John reports. *Oh my god, this is so exciting.*

She's making good time, Barrett texts.

Jack's worry settles. "She'll be waving a red bandana," he says. Then I get it. Ah yes, the red shirt. Pamplona. San Fermín. The running of the bulls.

A red speck in the distance grows into Caitlin, who a year ago decided to train for the nearly unattainable with her pony legs and fervent desire for things slightly beyond reach.

As she comes into focus, I see the bandana and huge red sunglasses. Caitlin is sporting Kinesio-taped legs to help hold together the various injuries she has sustained during her months of training, a professional job that from a distance makes her look like she's wearing patterned stockings. Her mouth wide open, she is nearly skipping up the left-hand side of the street toward us (*I run on the left, and plan to run on the left,* she had advised in her long, thoughtful pre-race email), waving her red flag, arms open, heading straight to her father, ostensibly to pick up an energy snack, but in reality to give him a hug before she runs on.

~

Some images stay with you for the rest of your life. You know it when they happen. Maybe you collect five of these over a lifetime.

We subway to Central Park, fight our way to the rail at mile 26. The first-wave runners are starting to appear. The party we witnessed in Brooklyn has morphed into a different gathering, with a somber, almost funereal tone. Many of the runners' once graceful, efficient forms have fallen apart. Their body language says it all: feet shuffling, trying to leave the earth as little as possible, overly active spastic arms trying to take over for the legs, some runners bent at the waist, upper bodies slightly ahead of the legs, collapsing toward the finish line. Most every one of them is struggling in some way. One runner is foaming at the mouth, another has a bloody face. Several are walking, gripping their cramping legs and sides. They have only two-tenths of a mile to go, and some cannot take another running step. We urge them on: "You can do it! You're doing it! You're almost there!" "Bravo Italia," Jack calls over and over. "Just a few more steps! Looking good!" I echo. We take direction from their running shirts: "Cassie, Brent, Jarrod, you go!" Some are still smiling, most grimacing in pain. A few glance our way when we call to them, a couple runners now walking look through me as if I can't possibly understand the horror.

We wait. My throat starts to hurt from all the screaming, and we wait. A few of the Achilles runners go by, pedaling recumbent bikes with their artificial limbs, in wheelchairs, or blind, all having started the race long before the others in their own special wave.

"She's slow," says Jack.

"Don't tell me that," I say. My heart is beating hard. I'm screaming my head off for the other runners. "You're almost there! Keep going! You're almost there!" All of a sudden, I'm screaming for Caitlin, I'm screaming for myself, for my ghosts, and for my competitive life, so fast running away from me. I'm screaming at the time left and lessons learned and courses run successfully, and those I failed at but was nonetheless successful in the trying. I'm yelling for my life and the lives of those I love, that I want so much to be imbued with meaning.

And there she is, still running on the left. Arduously now, but chugging along at a slow trot, still in decent-enough form, though the earlier glow is gone. She begins to make her way up the hill. Pushing and pushing, and still running. I position my camera. I scream and I scream. She glances over slowly and sees us, as if just moving her head to the left is too much effort—no smile, only the most essential movements—and then she looks again, her left arm raises, and she gives us a thumbs up as she trudges past us toward the finish. An anonymous runner on her right lifts his hand, touches her back in encouragement.

"I think she's hurting," I say to Jack.

"Of course," he says, "of course she's hurting."

~

Runners wrapped in their New York City Marathon tarps file past us, looking like bedraggled soldiers, or deflated angels, solemn, most with heads down, many limping, all walking impossibly slowly, their blue wings trailing behind them. We strain to catch our first glimpse of Caitlin but we will have to wait a long time for her to make it to us. But she does, eventually, still sporting the red dime-store glasses, consumed by the tarp and the completion medal she wears around her neck.

"I was slow," she will later complain. "My wall was a horrible cramp I got at mile 18 from drinking too much water. I had it for two miles. It finally went away at mile 20."

She bends her legs in place, trying to shake out the pain. A sea of blue around us.

"I learned all about cycles of pain, I can tell you that. And that what was bothering me before wasn't a problem. My knees and calves were fine, it was other stuff I least expected. My groin and stomach. I learned if I just kept running, the pain went away."

I try to hug her, but she recoils. Even *that* doesn't bother me.

"Please. Everything hurts," she says.

Her father and his wife leave for another engagement. We walk to the subway. People look at Caitlin and smile as she passes.

"You're a hero for a day in New York when you run the marathon."

We struggle to find correct change for the kiosk in the dungeon. One of the subway workers waves us through.

"Oh, that's so nice of you," I say.

My daughter frown-smiles and shakes her head under her blue hood. "They're supposed to do that for the runners," she explains.

We train back to Brooklyn and shuffle the few short blocks to her apartment. She finds she has forgotten to lock her door. We walk in, Caitlin admonishing herself, relieved to find her hole-in-the-wall is not a crime scene.

"Too bad I was so slow," she says again, stripping off the tarp, only half complaining, "but I finished my first marathon," she concludes, with some pride.

"I was thinking," she says to me after she has finally gotten off the phone with Barrett, "that in my career, where only twenty percent of female playwrights ever get produced and how awful the odds are to attain success, how cool is it that I set out to do something a little later in life that I'd never done before, and I did it. I actually did it." I smile to myself. *A little later in life? My almost thirty-year-old?*

"Caitlin, you're a marathon runner now."

The unattainable. I can feel that small frisson of excitement deep within me, and I open my hands for it.

Notes, 2022

He longs for her,
waking in the night, the way a lover might,

with the dead weight of something missing—
a daughter's love.
It has been years
since she talked to him.

She refuses to give in, the pain,
gnawing at a lung.
He believes he did nothing.
Which is exactly her complaint.

He and I, we don't talk much,
no longer pressure to relieve.
He sends photos so I will understand
the path he has chosen over mine—

his face ghosted in 21st story glass,
lit buildings, his painted cloth.
He says, "It's snowing in The City."
I ask, "How much?"

Northern Spies

We gathered wind-fallen apples for the horses—

hard little knots of promise,
    with brown, scaly blemishes.
        Kissed by the sun, my mother said.

My grandfather planted the gnarled trees, once saplings,
    on the hillside above Jackson Run,
        adjacent to the farmhouse.

I was too young to believe
        a body must be limbed for love;

that left to the elements,
    we rot, we scar. Still,
        the horses didn't know any better.

They devoured with foamy relish
    even the meanest of crabs,
        only good for our snowy palettes as pies or
        strudels—

or sauce gleaned from the apples
    best
        when it is still tart and warm, but barely.

Those un-tempting apples are my childhood.
  Buried deep in one,
        the worm of my mother wriggles to the
        surface;

a bathing cap still on
  and around her expanding midriff, a robe bound
        tight;
              her honeybee sunglasses

glinting the fallen world back to us
    in a field of a thousand mirrors.

Whitewashed to Look Made-of-Snow

A stone path, blushing
at its borders with bluebells and zinnias,

embellished the foreground of the farmhouse
as I skipped up the walk to the back door kitchen.

Then, when I had children of my own,
we came to visit grandparents,

tromping our snowy boots up the same stone steps,
Christmas lights winking at us from the house

where right was right and wrong was wrong.
We never used the front door,

tucked into a dark niche around the corner,
difficult to find for guests arriving

in burly winter coats and woolen scarves.
They usually gave up the ghost

and came through the Provence vapors of the kitchen.
As if the house were built and the road came after,

my own front door is also around back.
Maybe the architect wanted to keep

our comings and goings from the world.
Another generation goes by as I go with it

and I marvel how I am still stamped with
the starched ethics of what I came from

as well as a cattywampus farmhouse turned sideways,
limed and salted to look made-of-snow.

Fleeing For My Life

I still taste the sea
in these flat sandy plains of South Carolina.

No mountains to tempt me
but leagues of sugar sand in every direction,

leagues of sand, still plotting the sea.
I look back as I please.

I'd rather not know what's ahead,
breaking the knuckles on a pile of crab legs.

Even my daughter came into this world,
thanks to the sea within me.

Oh, how I'd rather look back—
as I slurp and squeeze the salty joints

of this life, with its bones
on the outside, smelling of the sea.

Cuttlefish

Their earliest photos
are sepia-toned,
even those dimmings from their adolescent years:
the one of Caitlin and John,
perched on the hearth's stone ledge
gazing up at their grandfather
as he quipped about cuttlefish—
the most intelligent invertebrate—
insisted on the morality
of the Vietnam War.

They were of an age
to be rapt, still,
in their grandfather's presence—
eight arms, brilliantly buoyant,
the last helicopter leaving Saigon.
They had yet to know the numbing of years,
after his death, after the photos faded,
except those trapped in the confines
of a palm-sized vertebrate,
having long ago walked out of the sea,
now tossed casually on some bamboo lounge
in bright sunlight, ringing.

Leaf Peeping

Water is rising,
and you don't know which way to run.
Your body hurts
and keeps hurting.
You start to take things away:
ambition, courage, desire.
Risk no longer sounds thrilling;
you are advised against taking it.
The horse, in his stall,
waits for the saddle.
The river gets dammed
before it meets the sea.
The fledgling falls out of her nest
before she is able to fly.
The old dog sleeps all day.
In a fit of rage, your daughter bobs
her waist-length hair.

This is the part
where it's too late to turn back.
The climbers are halfway up the mountain
and the snows are coming.
You push the pen across the page
with swollen fingers.
The soprano has a sore throat

and the understudy steps in.
The sun is sinking but it blazes hot.
Anthony Bourdain throws off the noose.
Sylvia Plath walks out of the kitchen.
Larry Levis stops drinking.
The old dog rouses for a limping walk.
Your daughter calls for advice.

The needle vibrates on a quarter tank,
as all your math
turns slowly to subtraction.
Time to hang up the spurs,
trim up the motor, shop for easy chairs,
make another meal of leftovers.
The trees have started to turn.
The horse opens his stride
on the bid toward home.
The snows are still coming,
and the climbers must find
a way down the mountain.
Find another way.

Take a car ride in the country
with your troubled daughter.
Admire the colors, the conversations
of the Ottauquechee River,
the kissing bridges,

connecting land to love.
Sit in the car without dancing,
though maybe she is dancing inside.
So much brilliance outside her window
is falling fast,
and the trouble is dancing.

August Outro

A pestering two-beat chirp—
a sound my mother warned
was the beginning of the end.
I was a young girl then,
long before I learned
the portent applied to me
and what comes achingly fast
then lingers.

My throat catches
on nectar drunk, decades eaten.
I jitter my legs, rub them together,
spread my human version
of a leathery wing.
I aim to have
ten thousand children.
I aim to attract you,
to pierce your ears
with my outro
and not let go.

Two Plates Instead of One

I choose four instead of three, three in lieu of the necessary
      two—
muscle memory superseding need.

One after the other, the children left
the plates behind.

Tonight, I take two plates out of my cupboard.
One day that will be too many.

Here, I'll say to your ghost,
would you care for an egg?

I'll poach it for you.

Acknowledgements

I am grateful to the following magazines and presses which first published these poems.

"History": *The Towson Flier*.

"Choice," "History," "Tilling the Grave" and "Adrift": *Fires at Yellowstone* (The Bacchae Press, 1993).

"In the Pasture of Dead Horses": *The Journal* and the *1995 Pushcart Anthology*.

"This Church": *The Louisville Review*.

"In the Pasture of Dead Horses," "This Church," "Tilling the Grave" and "Old Love": *Wheeler Lane* (Igneus Press, 1998).

"Once a Month He Gets the Kids": *Prairie Schooner, Scared Money Never Wins* (Finishing Line Press, 2004).

"Burning the Barn," "God Bless the Bid ": *Birmingham Poetry Review*.

"The Museum of Modern Art at 6 am": *Bayou*.

"Once a Month He Gets the Kids," "Burning the Barn," "The Museum of Modern Art at 6 am," and "God Bless the Bid": *Dark Track* (Word Tech Editions, 2005).

"The Get-a-way," "The Shower Cap": *Prairie Schooner*.

"Why I Love to Drink": *Southern Indiana Review*.

"Blue Stuff": *Nebraska Review*

"Something with Diamonds In It": *Confrontation*.

"The Get-a-way," "Why I Love to Drink," "The Shower Cap," "Blue Stuff," "Something with Diamonds In It," "The Art Project": *The Sorry Flowers* (Word Tech Editions, 2009).

"Mateus": *Gargoyle* ."Summoned": *JMWW*.

"Cream of Tartar," "Under the Influence," "Atlas" (Originally titled "Lists"), "Their Fantastic Mother," "Chocolate Sauce," Mateus," and "Summoned": *Take This Spoon* (Main Street Rag Press, 2014).

"It Came to Nothing": *Sloflopojo*.

"Shared Custody": *Cumberland Poetry Review*.

"The Anorexic Teaches Her Children": *The American Journal of Poetry*.

"Southpaw": *Cimarron Review*.

"Shared Custody," "The Anorexic Teaches Her Children," "Southpaw," Ripple Effect," and "Kites": *The Art of Falling* (FutureCycle Press, 2022).

"Owl": *As It Ought to Be*

"Northern Spies": *Summerset*

"August Outro": *Wild Roof*

"Nude Descending a Staircase": *The Bombay Literary Magazine*

Excerpt from *Finding My Distance* (Galileo Press, 2009)

"Twenty-Six Point Two": from *Come to the X* (Galileo Press, 2020)

Special thanks to Aswin Vijayan and Barrett Warner for their careful editing of this manuscript.

About the Author

Julia Wendell's sixth collection of poems, *The Art of Falling*, was published by FutureCycle Press in 2022. A Pushcart winner and recipient of Fellowships from Breadloaf and Yaddo, her poems have appeared widely in magazines such as *American Poetry Review, Missouri Review, Prairie Schooner, Cimarron Review*, and *Nimrod*. She is the Founding Editor of Galileo Press, lives in Aiken, South Carolina, and is a three-day event rider.

About the Press

Unsolicited Press is based out of Portland, Oregon and focuses on the works of the unsung and underrepresented. As a womxn-owned, all-volunteer small publisher that doesn't worry about profits as much as championing exceptional literature, we have the privilege of partnering with authors skirting the fringes of the lit world. We've worked with emerging and award-winning authors such as Shann Ray, Amy Shimshon-Santo, Brook Bhagat, Kris Amos, and John W. Bateman.

Learn more at unsolicitedpress.com. Find us on twitter and instagram.

www.ingramcontent.com/pod-product-compliance
Lightning Source LLC
Chambersburg PA
CBHW031426120626
46545CB00006B/2294